10 Tools for Authors

Julia A. Royston

BK Royston Publishing
P. O. Box 4321
Jeffersonville, IN 47131
502-802-5385
http://www.bkroystonpublishing.com
bkroystonpublishing@gmail.com

© Copyright – 2018

All Rights Reserved. No part of this book may be reproduced, stored in a retrieval system, or transmitted by any means without the written permission of the author.

Cover Design: Amit Designs

ISBN-13: 9781719877107

Printed in the United States of America

Dedication

I dedicate this book to anyone who has ever wanted to take the book you have and take it to the next level. You will eventually need tools, treasure and a team but start here. Let's go!

Acknowledgements

First, I acknowledge my Lord and Savior Jesus Christ for giving me all of my gifts and especially my gift to write His words.

My husband who is always supportive, loving and encouraging me to utilize all of my gifts and talents. Thank you honey.

To my mother, Dr. Daisy Foree, who is my number one cheerleader and always tells me, "hang in there, you can do it." To my father, Dr. Jack Foree, who is never far away from me in spirit or my heart. I only have to look in the mirror each day to see him.

To Rev. Claude and Mrs. Lillie Royston who support me in everything I do.

To the rest of my family, I love you and thank you for your prayers, support and love.

Introduction

At the printing of this book, I have been in business 10 years, written 50+ books and eBooks, published more than 100+ authors, coached just as many and seen others use my information to publish their own books. I am blessed beyond measure. I have seen things occur in my life that are beyond my wildest dreams. God said that he would 'exceed' all of my expectations. I am a witness that He did.

In my experience, I feel that it is my duty to share anything that I've learned. It's the teacher in me. I believe that no teacher should hold back secrets from students if it will help. I can't give away my secret sauce or recipe but if you watch close, be willing to invest, you will see the bread crumbs that I will leave behind. It is my honor, duty and legacy to all that has been given to me and placed in my hands.

There are many more tools that I can and maybe will write about but if you start with these 10, you'll be well on your way.

From the Author's Toolbox,
Julia

Tool #1

Mobile Phone

My father asked me did I want a mobile phone and I told him emphatically, "No!" Now, I don't what I would do without my phone. I literally can't live without my phone. I am highly productive with my phone. In addition to using a phone for its primary purpose, I conduct business on my phone. With the multiplicity of apps, I can send and receive invoices.

I can accept payments using multiple apps which helps my business stay afloat. Without money and profits, I would go out of business. Finally, I use my phone to communicate with my clients. I can send text messages, reply to social media inboxes and record videos.

I have a large storage capacity on my phone so I can live stream events, take wonderful pictures, upload the pictures or videos to the cloud and then share them with others. I can see others' videos via YouTube and be notified when a new video is uploaded or played.

I record messages to myself, book outlines and podcast/audio files via my phone. I can download, share or forward these audio files for sale, transcription and informational uses for my clients.

I can receive my emails from multiple email addresses so that I don't miss any important information. Having a reliable, affordable mobile phone is key to a successful business and writing is a business.

I realize that we don't like being tracked or feel like big brother is 'watching' but with children or elderly parents, the ability to track their whereabouts via the phone, can be helpful and give you peace and keep all of the pieces of your mind.

Phones are not just for making calls and receiving calls. Phones are an essential part of my life.

Get a great phone.

Important ways to use your phone.

- Set-up Voicemail with a Professional Message

- Subscribe to Google Phone is a unique number – separate from personal

- Load with Great Business Apps for better productivity

How do you use your phone?

Tool #2

Email

Email is not dead. Let's just clear the air on that up front. As much as we use other ways to communicate, email is still a viable tool to communicate. Besides send basic messages, email is used to send professional documents and other information.

You can use email for marketing, promotional and announcements or flyers about your upcoming book or new business service.

Know that email can be used in a court of law with the date, time stamp and actual receipt of the email from one party to the next. Any incriminating or defamatory information sent via email can be held up in court as well.

In the signature area of an email, helpful, marketing and promotional information should be placed there. Email represents you and your brand. Use email wisely. I have seen people lose their jobs and positions over the misuse of email.

As much as email can be a useful, profitable and promotional tool, used in the wrong way and for the wrong purposes can come with harmful results and reprimands.

Remember:

- Your name or brand at the beginning of email
    - doejane@gmail.com
    - yourfamousbooktitle@gmail.com
- Professional Signature with Contact information
- Check on a regular basis
- Respond to it promptly
- Strictly for Business Transactions and Communication

How do you still use email?

Start an Email List

Tool #3

Laptop or Tablet

I confess that I am a geek, nerd or techno lover. I confess it so you don't have to accuse me of it. I am a creative, productive business person so having the right tools to do what I love is critical. Fortunately for me, I am married to a man that is an even bigger technology nut than I am. He loves technology and realizes the importance of me having the best, latest and fastest technology available. Man, am I so thankful for that man. Yes!

On the other hand, it is a sacrifice that I make to have the latest technology. Why? Technology is crucial to how I live and what I do. If I didn't make it a priority, I would spend my money on something else, somewhere else. I need it, so I spend money on it. Finally, with the good technology, I am able to produce more, not lose documents and become even more profitable which in the long run is a win/win situation all of the way around.

With that being said, having the ability to be mobile with a laptop or other device that is reliable, is key for me. My presentations, recordings and display materials for sales are done much better if I have a laptop.

If you don't know what to buy, reach out to me and my husband will strive to help. He is an IT/tech guy for more than 30 years. Go to http://bit.ly/talkwithroyston to schedule an appointment. Any questions, email us at bkroystonpublishing@gmail.com and put 'help with technology' in the subject line. Let's go!

Remember

- Android Tablet or Apple iPad
- Compare the two and pick one
- Provides tools like a desktop but mobile
- Multiple access points – phone and tablet

What type of laptop do you have and do you use it all of the time?

_____
_____
_____
_____
_____
_____
_____

Tool #4

CANVA.com

Canva is one of those free tools that I don't know how I came to live without. Canva is a graphic design tools that allows you to create basic and elaborate graphics for your book, business or non-profit organization. There are handy templates, shapes, images, fonts and other guidance to help you create great graphics. At times, you don't have the money or time to search for a graphic designer but have to have a graphic completed in a hurry. Canva is the tool.

There are additional paid images, templates and tools but the majority of the graphics can be created with the free tools provided for you.

Because I am an avid social media user, there are templates for specific social media platforms that are already sized for you. In addition to social media templates, there are templates for ebooks, posters, brochures, pamphlets and stationary among a variety of other templates.

I have had professional and experienced graphic designers use it in addition to the other graphics tools that they use to design and create. Don't sleep on Canva. It can get you out of a lot of situations where graphics is needed in a hurry.

Sign up for Canva today!

Create a free canva.com account. Create a simple graphic for a book, product or service.

_____
_____
_____
_____
_____
_____
_____
_____
_____
_____
_____
_____
_____
_____

Tool #5

Video Communication

If a picture is worth a thousand words, then a video is worth a million. Videos have become extremely an important part of marketing, promotion and business communication. It is the fastest growing area of marketing and promotion in business today. Today, it is not a choice of whether you will have a video or not but how what will be the subject of your next video?

Todays videos do not have to be professionally done or complicated. The phone has advanced technologically that the camera on the phone rivals most digital cameras that cost hundreds of dollars.

You may have one very involved, professionally edited and produced video but clients, audiences and customers today crave video communication. They don't just want to see your words but they want to see and hear you. They want a greater experience of being connected with you. For me, I produce a short 60 second video via Instagram every single day. I go live with Facebook LIVE with major webinars, announcements or other information that I want to produce. I also have promotional videos that I produce specifically for my business as well as book trailers for my books.

Video sells books. Videos give life to books and make you more human and relatable to your audiences.

Words have power. Picture leave a lasting impression but video stays with people even longer and leave an immovable imprint on people lives.

What will you share with your readers, clients or customers today?

Challenge: Open your phone and record a video of this information in 2-5 minutes. Let's go!

_____
_____
_____
_____
_____
_____
_____
_____
_____
_____
_____
_____
_____
_____
_____
_____
_____

Tool #6

Business Social Media Page

I don't know whether you know it or not but the way that you communicate with followers and other users with social media changes often. Why? Because the needs of the followers, the financial results and/or potential for profitability of the owners change and the ability to control and manipulate what we can and cannot do on social media can fluctuate at will.

Why have a business social media page? I'm glad you asked. First, the algorithm has changed for posting from posting sites such as Hootsuite.com or IFFFTT to only posting to business social media pages and not personal pages. Secondly, my current objective now on my business pages is to get people to sign up to get access to my email list or visit my website for more information.

Thus, I have a business social media page on Facebook, LinkedIN, Instagram or Twitter and the graphics, texts and/or other shared videos all have a link to a form, landing page or website for more information or to gain access to my Internet real estate.

So if you don't have a business, what do you do? Set up a business profile page as an author, public figure, etc. Don't delete your personal page and don't stop posting things about your books, events and/or other helpful and positive posts but know that with the ever-changing rules of social media, be ready to collect and have your own list, just in case.

First exercise is to always collect business cards at events. Be sure to give a business card as you are collecting. Keep it fair. When you are having/hosting/attending events as a vendor, keep a journal or notebook or pad of paper to begin developing a list of people for future events.

_____
_____
_____
_____
_____
_____
_____
_____
_____
_____

Bonus: I always have some type of give a way or freebie at events to also collect information from people. Your own information gathering exercises are key to building your brand by having your own list.

What's Your Give-a-way?

_____

_____

_____

_____

_____

_____

_____

_____

_____

Create a business or public figure profile on your social media outlet of choice.

Tool #7

Email Marketing Service

Email marketing is a way that you market your business, book, products and services to an audience that has voluntarily signed up for to be on your email list. Your purpose is to build relationships, establish trust, give important information and then see if the people on the list are interested in more information, other products, and services, attend a live event, conference, workshop or retreat. This is done simply through email.

There are several email marketing systems around but the one that I use the most is GetResponse. There are others such as Constant Contact, Mailerlite and many others. These systems have the ability to collect emails from forms, newsletters and or other interactive documents. Once the email address is received, there can be communication sent back to the email address holder via newsletter, autoresponders, simple email messages and other forms.

The email address holder can decide whether they want to continue to be a subscriber or unsubscribe to your services based on the information provided.

One of the major reasons to have an email marketing services is because you need your own personal list of clients and customers instead of having a social media third party. In the event that the social media platform ends, you have a way to communicate with people directly and not just communicate through a third-party vendor. Companies cease to exist every day. Be sure that you have a way to communicate with your clients directly.

Check your budget and needs for an email marketing system and ask Uncle Google what the top 10 email marketing systems are and do your own homework.

_____
_____
_____
_____
_____
_____
_____
_____
_____
_____
_____
_____
_____
_____
_____

Tool #8

Payment Methods

If you have no money in your business, you will soon be out of business. Also, there is nothing worse than not being able to accept payment with the method that your client/customer wants to give it to you. In the end, you miss out on a sale and lower your bottom line for that event. I remember so clear being at an event and my friend walked away from her table and I agreed to watch it for her.

I knew the costs of the products she was selling. There was a woman who wanted to buy 4 of her books. My friend did not accept credit cards at the time. I did. I received the money for her and paid her the money for her books later. My friend was eternally grateful but that was the last time that she didn't accept credit cards at a live event.

Are you able to receive credit card payments for your products and services?

At a recent event, there was an issue with receiving credit cards on the company's end and not me.

Fortunately, I had another credit card app that I could receive credit card payments. So, not only do I accept credit cards with one company but 3 companies. Why? Because what if one company is hacked, server is down or the app will not work. One company shouldn't stop my money flow. As my grandfather said, 'what one won't do, another one will.' Make sure that other one is a great credit card company app.

How many ways/companies/apps are you able to receive payments for your products and services?

Tool #9

Website

There is nothing like having your own place. Whether it's your first apartment, condo, townhouse, trailer or mansion, it's yours! Nothing can stop you but you from maintaining it, fixing it up, redecorating or selling it and moving out. It's yours.

The same is with a website. It's your own piece of Internet real estate. You can dress it up as elaborate or as minimal as you want. Have a 3-page website or a 25-page website, it doesn't matter because it is yours. What if your favorite social media site closed down tomorrow? What would you do? Where would you send people to find out information about you, your goods and services, communicate with you and upcoming events? That's what your website does. It is your house and your residence for all things you and about you.

Finally, a website is like a child or house, it must be maintained, revised, updated and revamped from time to time to stay current. A website is not a one-time setup and put on auto-pilot. A website is a living, breathing and evolving entity.

Some basic things that you should be on a website:

- Biographical Information
- Contact Information with a form for accepting email addresses
- Professional photos
- Event information
- Product and Service information
- Grammatically correct introduction and welcome to

those who will visit your website.

Tool #10

Cloud/Off-Site Storage

Cloud storage or off-site storage is like insurance, you need to have it before you need. There is nothing like having your laptop or desktop computer crash and you lose all of your documents, books or other confidential information and it can't be retrieved. For 22 years, I was an educator, media specialist and most of the time, the technology coordinator for 2 schools. I have seen the anguish of teachers and administrators when their documents could not be retrieved because they forgot to save them, back them up or have a duplicate copy in cloud storage or external drive.

You used to have to be a major tech geek to have external drives to save your information but now, it is as easy as going to Walmart, Best Buy or other online tech store and purchase a plug external drive to store your data. Additionally, with a Google account, you have access to 15 gigabytes of storage, which is a lot, for documents, videos and audio files and you can purchase more. This is called and considered cloud storage. Meaning that you can access this information from any computer in the world as long as you are logged into your email account. The information is not on your computer but in an off-site cloud storage. Cloud storage may sound strange but if you have ever lost your documents, you will figure out a way to never have this happen to you again.

Now, the most important thing is that once you have a cloud storage account, you need to regularly store your documents there. Having an account and using it, is two different things. I have seen people do that too. They still save their documents to their hard drive and have the off-site storage but never save the documents on the off-site storage. When the computer crashes they are disappointed in the cloud base storage because it didn't miraculously know that you had documents that you wanted to save there. It doesn't work like that. Get in the habit of creating documents on whatever platform you want, then saving and storing documents to your off-site storage.

Exercise: Go to Uncle Google again, ask him for the top 10 cloud storage sites. If they look too technical for you, try Google Drive or Dropbox. Create accounts and start saving your documents. Let's go!

_____

_____

_____

_____

_____

_____

_____

_____

_____

_____

www.ingramcontent.com/pod-product-compliance
Lightning Source LLC
Chambersburg PA
CBHW031550210526
45464CB00003B/1234